Spot Goes Clip, Clop

Written by
Debbie Strayer

Illustrations by
Joy Majewski

New Sounds:

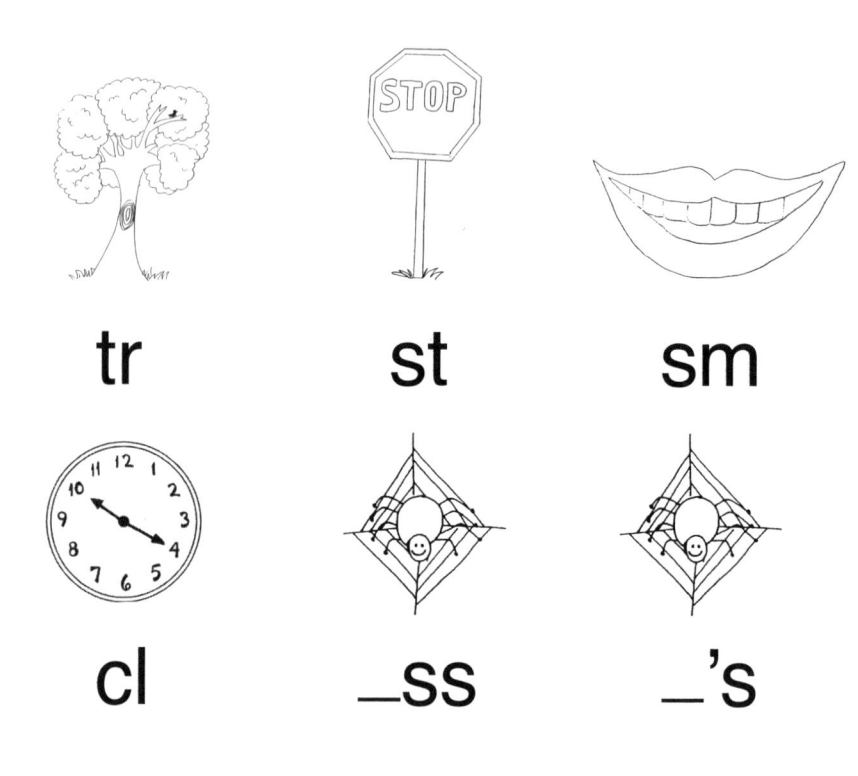

tr   st   sm

cl   _ss   _'s

(Note: The pictures indicate the sound, not the spelling.)

Common Sense Press

© 1998 by Common Sense Press

Printed 09/15

8786 Highway 21 • Melrose, FL 32666

ISBN 1-880892-59-6

Sam calls Spot.
Spot likes to trot.

1

Here is Spot's stall.
He can fit. He is small.

Pam calls Sam. The food in the pot is hot.

Sam and Pam sit.
Time for all to eat.

Spot ate in his stall.
He bit the grass.

Ham and yams are in the pot. Yum! Then they can have jam.

The wall in the hall is tall. They can not see Spot as he goes clip, clop.

Silly Spot! He is not a tot! Sam and Pam love Spot.

New Words:

tr	cl	st	sm	__ss	__'s
trot	clip	stall	small	grass	Spot's
	clop				

Spot	bit	Sam
tot	fit	Pam
pot	sit	ham
		jam
		yams

New Sight Words:

food	time	eat	as	ate
goes	then	love	silly	

Word Family:

-all

all

stall

small

wall

hall

tall

calls

Review Words:

here	is	not	and	see
are	his	hot	can	they
in	to	he	the	for
have	a	likes		